PETS

PETS

BY ALICE FIELDS
Illustrated by Frankie Coventry

An Easy-Read Fact Book

FRANKLIN WATTS
New York/London/Toronto/Sydney/1981

The author and publisher would like to thank the following for permission to reproduce photographs:
Marc Henrie; William McQuitty; Mansell Picture Library

Library of Congress Cataloging in Publication Data

Fields, Alice.
  Pets.

  (An Easy-read fact book)
  Includes index.
  SUMMARY: Basic information for the young child about deciding to have a pet, choosing a pet, and caring for a pet.
  1. Pets—Juvenile literature. [1. Pets] I. Title.
SF416.F53   636.08′87   80-20281
ISBN 0-531-04188-3

R.L. 2.9 Spache Revised Formula

All rights reserved
Printed in the United Kingdom
6 5 4 3 2 1

For thousands of years, people have kept pets.
Probably the first animals to be tamed were dogs. They were used for hunting.

The picture above shows a carving made several thousand years ago.

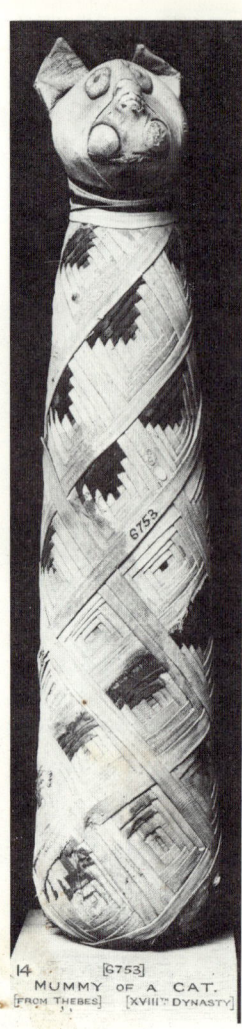

**Left: statue of a cat that was worshiped by ancient Egyptians.
Right: the Egyptians sometimes preserved cats in mummy form.**

Later, cats were tamed to be pets. The Egyptians used cats as objects of worship.

Songbirds were kept in China as long as two thousand years ago. They appear in many old Chinese paintings and drawings.

Bird sellers in a Chinese market

Today, dogs, cats, and birds are still the most popular pets.

Cats and dogs that live together in the same house can get along well with each other. They do not have to be enemies.

Some people keep unusual animals as pets.

Having an exotic pet might be fun. But you cannot go shopping with a snake coiled around your neck...

or a large monkey riding on your back...

or a lion on a leash.

Just think of some of the problems in keeping such creatures.

young chimp

For instance, monkeys have delicate health and can sometimes be very vicious.

lion cub

Lions become large and powerful, and can be very dangerous.

A lion would probably eat more meat than your whole family could eat.

Most countries have laws that forbid people to keep wild animals as pets.

Wild animals are much better off in their natural homes. There they have the right climate, food, and exercise to meet their needs.

You do not have to live in a jungle to see wild animals, though.

Squirrels, toads, and mice may live in your own backyard. Beavers, rabbits, and raccoons may live in the countryside near you.

If you are thinking of getting a pet, it is best to choose one that is...

easy to tame...

gray rabbit

adult guinea pigs

Many pets like company. A guinea pig or two and a rabbit get along well together.

not too expensive to feed...

14

easy to keep clean...

Hamsters in their cage

the right size for the space you have.

Big dogs need room to exercise and run about.

So if you live in an apartment or small house, a St. Bernard or a Great Dane might not be a good idea.

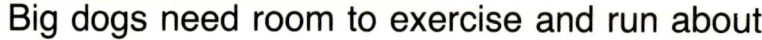

Great Dane

This picture shows some of the fish you can keep at home. Goldfish must be kept in a cold-water tank. Tropical fish need a heated tank.

There might be room for a goldfish tank or a birdcage. And a small dog, like a poodle or a Scottie, doesn't need much space.

17

Before you decide what kind of pet to buy, you should answer one question--honestly. Will you look after it every single day?

Any animal you get will be dependent on you for...
food and water...

boxer

exercise...

comfort and cleanliness...

love and affection.

A boarding kennel can be a busy place during vacation time.

Keeping a pet is a full-time job. Is there someone to care for it while you are at school? And what about your vacation? You may have to make an arrangement with a kennel, or a pet-sitter.

These boys are choosing a guinea pig.

A large pet shop is a good place to visit. There you will see all kinds of animals--some can be kept indoors, others in the garden.

Such a visit can help you decide just which kind of pet to buy. At a pet shop, you can also find out the costs of buying and keeping different pets.

It's a good idea to plan ahead before you buy your pet.

Get a book about the animal from the library. Learn all you can about its care and habits before you get it home.

Libraries have books and information on many subjects.

You can buy water conditioner to add to the tank water. This shortens the time needed for the water to settle.

Just as your home is important to you, so is a proper home for your pet.

Fish, for example, should not be bought before you have arranged a tank for them. The water needs to settle for two or three days.

Be certain the pet you buy is healthy.

A puppy should be full of life, not quiet and sad. Its eyes should be clear and its nose cold and wet.

cocker spaniel puppy

long-haired kitten

A kitten should be lively, without any sign of a cold. Its nose should be cool.

Guinea pigs should have full coats, big bright eyes, and strong-looking teeth.

Abyssinian guinea pig (top)
smooth-haired guinea pig (top right)

Himalayan rabbit (front)

brown rabbit (back)

A rabbit's ears should be inspected for mites or infections. If it is sneezing, or showing other signs of a cold, do not buy it.

A turtle should not have a cracked shell or a runny nose.

turtle

Birds should seem lively and alert and have smooth, shiny feathers.

parakeet

canary

Ask the pet shop dealer about caring for and feeding your new pet.

You will soon learn how much food your pet needs. It is important not to overfeed it.

Your pet must have fresh water at all times.

The charts on the next four pages will give you an idea of the special needs of different pets.

Try and make the animal's home as nearly like its natural home as you can.

Pet	Home	Food	Special Needs

Puppies — Basket for sleeping, with high sides to keep out cold air. Put a blanket on bottom of basket. — Milk, cereal, soft foods at first. Finely cut-up meat once a week for 3 months, then more often. — By age 3 months, all puppies should be inoculated against distemper, rabies, and hepatitis.

Kittens — Basket for sleeping, with high sides to keep out cold air. Put a blanket on bottom of basket. — Milk. Finely cut-up fish and meat. At about 6 months, three-fourths of diet should be meat and fish. — Kittens should be inoculated against feline infectious enteritis and feline distemper.

Pet	Home	Food	Special Needs

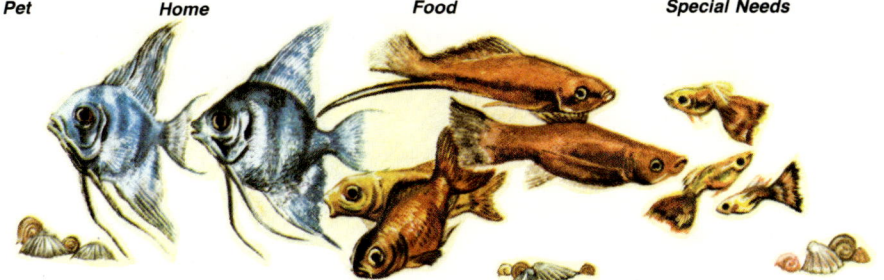

Fish — Tank. Should contain water, gravel, rocks, and plants. Tank should be protected from strong sunlight, but lit with an electric light to allow plants to give off oxygen. A heating unit is needed for tropical fish. | Prepared fish food, and live food. Both are available from pet shops. | Tank should be completely prepared and allowed to settle for 2 or 3 days before fish are placed in it. Use of a water-conditioner cuts down the time needed for water to settle.

Birds — Cages, of different sizes and shapes depending on kind of bird. Should be placed away from cold air and contain a small "bath." | Most feed on various kinds of seeds that can be bought from pet shops or markets. Greens and meal worms are also important. Some birds (myna) need ripe fruit. | It is often better to keep two birds, as one tends to get lonely.

29

Pet	Home	Food	Special Needs

Tortoises

Often die from cold weather, so hibernation details are especially important.

Wire pen with shelter at one end. Need direct sunshine, not through glass. Allow to sunbathe in the yard in a pen with wire cover.

Grass, leaves of lettuce, cabbage, and dandelion. Tomatoes, soft fruit. Bone meal against calcium deficiency.

Tortoises hibernate in winter. They should be put in a deep box with leaves and hay on bottom. Cover box with mesh netting. Leave box in a cool place.

Turtles

Are very difficult to keep alive. If kept, proper food and sunshine are essential.

Tank with rocks and plants. Allow to sunbathe in yard in container with wire cover to guard against cats.

Lean meat, garden worms, raw fish, water insects.

Turtles cannot breathe underwater, so tank should only be half-filled with water and not covered with glass.

Grass Snakes

Glass tank with wire mesh top, containing branches, some large stones, and "pond" of water.

Toads, frogs, tadpoles, small fish, water insects, raw meat.

Grass snakes hibernate in winter. Place in a tin with holes in lid, on a bed of moss and leaves. Leave in a cool place. Do not disturb until spring.

Pet	Home	Food	Special Needs
Rabbits 	Hutch (pen) large enough for rabbit to stand up comfortably. Separate sleeping compartment.	Dry grass and greens. Lettuce, cabbage, and dandelion leaves. A mash of bran, oats, and meal.	Rabbits should be kept in separate hutches, or in pairs if you wish to breed. When a female is pregnant, move her to her own hutch.
Hamsters 	Metal cage. Should have exercise wheel, or pet should be allowed to run free each day.	Leafy vegetables, grains, fruit, nuts.	The safest rule is "one hamster, one cage." Two together will fight with each other.
Guinea Pigs 	Pen or cage with sleeping area, and room for animal to run about.	Greens, carrots, celery, grass, oats.	Males and females should be separated when about a month old, to prevent breeding.
Mice/Rats 	Metal cages (larger for rats) with two levels, or with some means of exercise.	Seeds, vegetables, dry bread.	Both rats and mice breed very rapidly. Separate males and females if you do not wish them to breed.

Do not pick up a rabbit by its ears alone. You may hold it by its ears and its rump.

Once you have your pet home, you must learn to handle it.

Let it get used to you--your sound and smell--before touching it a lot.

Your pet will probably be nervous and feel strange at first.

Talk to it softly. Allow it to explore and get used to its new home.

Never grab an animal. Pick it up as carefully as you would a baby.

When you feed an animal, be sure to hold your hand flat with the food in the palm of your hand.
This is the safest way. Some animals will bite or peck at fingers holding food.

Feeding a young donkey

Cat using a litter box

    Dogs and cats have to be housebroken.

    Puppies can be trained to use newspapers. As soon as the puppy shows signs of wanting to relieve itself, place it on some newspaper.

    Kittens soon learn to use a litter box. Always keep the box in the same place. Firmly but gently, take the cat to the box. Cats take pride in keeping clean and neat.

    Remember, pets are like people. Shouting will make them nervous. Making a fuss over them when they learn will make them happy.

Teach your dog to sit while you wait to cross the street.

When a dog is very young, it should be trained to be obedient.

You can teach your dog to come when its name is called. It can learn to "sit" and "stay." Dogs probably don't much like the word "down," but they can learn what it means. They should also be taught to take a walk with you without pulling on the leash.

It takes time and patience to train a dog, but it's worth it. A poorly trained dog is no fun as a pet.

If you want help in learning how to train your dog, find a book at the library on dog care.

Or, if you have special problems, there are obedience schools for dogs in many cities.

A dog obedience class

A pet needs care every single day.

How would you feel if your mother forgot to feed you one day? You would probably start feeling very sorry for yourself.

You might also become ill from hunger.

A pet is a living creature. It needs almost as much care as you do.

Cats like soft things for beds. This one is made of cloth.

Some different types of guinea pigs

Fresh water and food are necessary, usually twice a day.

Food should not be left standing for too long. It can spoil or get dirty.

All food and water containers need to be carefully washed each day.

Dutch rabbit

 Most animals are naturally clean creatures. You may notice that a rabbit, for instance, usually soils only one corner of its hutch. The rest is kept free of droppings.

It is most important, for your pet's health and comfort, to keep its home clean.

If you can, buy tray-type flooring for the cage. The tray can then be removed each day. It should be washed in hot water and thoroughly dried. The old bedding should be discarded, and replaced with clean.

Most animals need some sort of bedding. Hay, newspapers, or sawdust are the most common types. A pet dealer can tell you the type you need.

Left: when cleaning a cage, tip the dirty litter onto paper and throw it away. Right: the cage must be washed with soap and hot water. If you use a disinfectant, be sure that it is safe for animals.

Left: returning a hamster to its clean cage. Right: always wash your hands before and after cleaning your pet's cage.

Always wash your hands thoroughly after cleaning out cages, removing dirty bedding, or touching your pet's food.

It is very important that you keep as clean as possible when handling animals. Diseases can sometimes be passed from animals to humans.

Does your cat or dog roam around in the neighborhood or woods? You don't really know what your pet might come in contact with.

Play it safe. It's a bother to always be washing your hands—but do it!

All animals need exercise. They get very bored without it.

Dogs should be taken for daily walks. If possible, they should also be allowed to run free for a time.

Let your bird fly about a room. Be sure all doors and windows are tightly shut.

Your pet will also enjoy a special toy that you can buy it.

parakeet

collie

mongrel

silver tabby cat

Never try to treat a sick animal yourself.

When you first get your pet, locate the nearest animal doctor, or veterinarian. Then if your pet gets sick, you know where to take it right away.

Today, many animal diseases can be prevented by vaccinations.

These young puppies are suckling their mother's milk.

Keeping a pet involves a lot of time and care. It may seem like a lot of trouble at times. But there are rewards.

You will be able to study an animal firsthand. You can learn all about its habits and life cycle. You may have the fun of helping your pet look after its babies.

Dogs are also excellent as protection against trouble.

Many pets have a lot of love and affection to give their owners.

Treat an animal kindly, and it will return all the love you give it.

This farmhand is feeding the cows.

Some people find animals so interesting that they decide to work with them. You might decide to work on a farm, or be a veterinarian. Maybe you would like to breed dogs or own a riding stable. You could work in a pet shop or become a jockey.

There are many careers that involve animals. Having a pet might be a learning opportunity for the future.

INDEX

Beds, 28, 38, 41
Birds
    care required, 29, 43
    choosing, 26
Breeding, 31

Cages for
    birds, 29, 41–42
    guinea pigs, 31, 41–42
    hamsters 31, 41–42
    mice and rats, 31, 41–42
Cats
    care required, 28, 35, 38
    choosing, 24
    housebreaking, 35
    kittens, 24, 28, 35
    vaccinations, 28

Distemper, 28
Dogs
    care required, 28, 35–37, 45
    choosing, 16–17, 24
    puppies, 24, 28, 35, 45
    training, 35–37
    vaccinations, 28

Enteritis, 28

Exercise, 16, 19, 31, 43

Fish
    care required, 17, 23, 29, 33
Food requirements, 19, 27, 34, 38–39
    birds, 29
    cats, 28
    dogs, 28
    guinea pigs, 31
    hamsters, 31
    mice and rats, 31
    rabbits, 31
    snakes, 30
    tortoises, 30
    turtles, 30

Guinea Pigs
    care required, 31
    choosing, 25

Hamsters, 31
Handling pets, 32–33, 42
Hibernation, 30

Illness, 28, 42, 44

Mice, 13, 31

Mites, 25

Pens. See also *Cages*.
    for rabbits, 31, 40–42
    for tortoises, 30

Rabbits
    care required, 31, 32
    choosing, 25
Rabies, 28
Rats, 31

Snakes, 8, 30

Tanks for,
    fish, 17, 23, 29
    snakes, 30
    turtles, 30
Tortoises, 30
Turtles
    care required, 30
    choosing, 26

Vaccinations, 28, 44

Water, 19, 23, 27, 39
Wild animals, 8-13

SUMMIT LIBRARY